Dragons are commonly thought to have magical or supernatural powers and are usually shown as huge, winged, fire-breathing reptiles. They appear in many cultures and religions with body parts taken from different animals and birds.

In 2004, a skull was found in Hell Creek, South Dakota. It had a dragonlike head, horns, and teeth, so it was called Dracorex hogwartsia *after Hogwarts School from the Harry Potter stories.*

DRAGONS OF THE FAR EAST

Japanese dragons are similar to Chinese dragons but have three claws instead of four. They are usually kind, associated with water, and may grant you wishes.

The Chinese Dragon Dance …

… is a highlight of Chinese New Year celebrations. People dance through the stre carrying poles holding up an image of a dra

In Asian cultures, the dragon is a heavenly being. It is treated as a wonderful and powerful creature, protecting people and nations.

Chinese dragon symbolizes ngth and is often linked to luck. The Chinese Emperor used mperial dragon symbol on his hes, furniture, and buildings how his power. The dragon ears in other Asian cultures and is etimes called the Oriental dragon. a long, snakelike creature with claws (or five for the Imperial gon). Many pictures show a creature made up of erent animal parts, such as fins or scales of a fish and the is of a deer.

According to an ancient myth, the Vietnamese people are descended from the magical union of a dragon king and a fairy. This large-jawed dragon brings rain to help farmers and their crops. It also represents the emperor, and the wealth and power of the nation.

Vietnamese Dragon

5

DRAGONS OF THE FAR EAST

Dragons featured in folk stories and myths have been brought into the 21st Century with movie special effects and computer imaging.

Viking stories featured fantastic characters, such as trolls and el[ves], as well as dragons. These dragons were said to live in the underground world and at the bottom of the ocean.

VIKING
LEGENDS

Sigurd is a Norse hero, famous for slaying (killing) dragons in north European myths from long ago.

Vikings decorated the front of their ships with dragons to scare off sea monsters.

Viking mythology features some great dragons, such as Fafnir, killed by Sigurd; Jörmungandr, enemy of Thor; and Nithhogr, who ate the dead! Vikings believed in nine worlds, all linked by a giant tree called Yggdrasil. A mighty dragon named Nidhogg gnawed at the tree's roots.

Ice Dragons are pale, crystal colors, such as white or icy blue. Their weapon is not a blast of fire, but a burst of freezing wind containing jagged ice crystals.

Jörmungandr *is a giant sea dragon that was thrown into the ocean by Odin. The monster grew big enough to reach around the earth and grasp its own tail. The legend says the world will end when it lets go. Thor catches the creature using an ox head as bait, but the giant, Hymir is so frightened that he cuts the dragon free.*

In Viking legend, Fafnir,
a magician's son, changed
into a dragon because he was
very greedy. He guarded his hoard
of treasures with his fiery breath.

VIKING
LEGENDS

3-D WILD WORLD

DRAGONS

PANORAMA

Are you brave enough to open these pages and face the ultimate 3D dragon encounter?

EUROPEAN DRAGON LORE

Many medieval heroes had to fight and kill a dragon, as in the story of St. George. There are more great dragons in the legends of King Arthur, who was the son of Uther Pendragon (which means head or chief dragon).

ragons in European folklore are seen as a bad force, nlike the great dragons of the East. They often have ard skin or armor and wings, although they don't always fly. They breathe fire and can destroy crops or prey on humans, taking children or women as hostages in return for gold and food.

This stamp shows St. George the dragon slayer. He is the patron saint of several countries, including England, Russia, India, Greece, and Portugal.

The people of Wales are proud of their red dragon. It is on the Welsh flag with a green and white background.

In Celtic mythology, four dragons represent the four ancient elements: Earth, Fire, Air, and Water. The Fire Dragon stands for bravery and energy.

The Druids were ancient priests and were seen as fortune tellers. For them, dragons were powerful symbols that meant a good harvest was to come. Lightning was a sign that dragons roamed nearby, and the next year would be a lucky one.

Some dragons breathe fire but others were said to be venomous, such as in the Old English poem, *Beowulf*.

EUROPEAN DRAGON LORE

MODERN MONSTERS

Dragon tales have changed through the centuries. While they were once seen as fearsome and powerful, many modern stories simply cast them as the bad guys. The mythical Vikings learn how to slay them in the movie *How to Train Your Dragon*, and the competitors in the Triwizard tournament of the Harry Potter stories have to defeat ferocious dragons to reach the next stage of the competition.

This is a traditional Ukrainian folk dragon. One such dragon is defeated by Ivanko in an old folk tale.

Harry Potter comes face to face with a Hungarian Horntail, the most dangerous dragon in the Triwizard tournament. The other dragons are a Swedish Short-snout, a Common Welsh Green, and a Chinese Fireball. They are all bad-tempered, fire-breathing beasts with an assortment of vicious claws, tail, horns, and razor-sharp teeth.

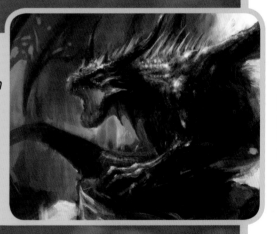

The biggest of the dragons reach more than six tons (5.5 tonnes). They fly clumsily, despite their huge wingspan.

Some dragons have a frill or hood, like a cobra. The Indian dragon, Nāga is one of these. Many dragons are huge, but some are tiny, like fire lizards from Anne McCaffrey's Dragonriders of Pern series of books.

MODERN MONSTERS

Dragons are often described as reptiles with scaly bodies and long tails. They are usually said to hatch from eggs. Many movie dragons look a lot like dinosaurs, and scientists hundreds of years ago, believed that fossilized bones they found belonged to real-life dragons.

REAL LIFE DRAGONS

A living dragon: the Komodo dragon from Indonesia.

The Komodo dragon is a giant species of lizard with many dragonlike features, includir a venomous bite. They live on a handful of islands in Indonesia and can grow to 10 feet (3 m) long. They are strong enough to kill humans, but eat deer and wild pigs. Fortunately, they don't fly or breathe fire!

Building Birdhouses & Feeders

This book contains 12 birdhouse and 12 bird feeder designs ranging from simple to complex. Some are traditional, some are rustic, and some are whimsical. Each project is described in clearly written step-by-step instructions and detailed plans.

$7.95 U.S.

ISBN 0-89721-21

0 71549 05982 8